Loving Someone with Depression

A Guide to Understanding, Supporting, and Nurturing Through the Darkness

Rachel J. Oles

Table of Contents

INTRODUCTION

Depression, a ubiquitous mental health illness, throws a deep shadow on the lives of individuals and their relationships. In this exploration, we look into the ubiquity of depression, its far-reaching influence on both persons and relationships, and the personal motivation fueling the creation of this guide.

Recognizing the necessity of assisting a loved one through the darkness of depression is not only an awareness of their struggle but an active commitment to promoting understanding, resilience, and compassion.

Depression is a widespread mental health disease, impacting millions of individuals worldwide. According to the World Health Organization (WHO), over 264 million individuals suffer from depression, making it a primary cause of disability globally. The incidence of depression stretches beyond age, gender, and socio-economic lines, underscoring its indiscriminate character. From the weight of constant melancholy to the immobilising consequences on daily functioning, depression's influence is substantial and far-reaching.

In relationships, the existence of depression adds an extra layer of complexity. Partners, family members, and friends are dragged into the orbit of the individual's suffering, navigating the emotional turbulence that characterises the landscape of depression. Understanding the ubiquity of depression is vital for debunking the notion that it is an unusual or isolated experience, developing empathy, and paving the way for constructive support.

Behind every written word is a personal drive, a driving force that propels an author to go on the journey of developing a book like "Loving Someone with Depression." For me, the inspiration derives from a very personal connection to the subject matter.

Witnessing a loved one navigate the maze of despair, I found myself battling with doubts, anxieties, and a desire to be a beacon of support. This book is developed out of the knowledge that, in the face of sadness, love can be both a tremendous force and a delicate thread that demands careful weaving.

The motivation extends beyond the personal, recognizing the social need for services that give a sympathetic hand to people navigating the complicated dance with depression. The significant influence that mental health difficulties can have on relationships spurred the discovery of solutions, insights, and viewpoints that could serve as a guiding light for those walking similar roads.

Importance of Supporting a Loved One during Depression

Supporting a loved one through depression is not a passive act; it is an active commitment to understanding, patience, and unflinching compassion. The importance of this assistance cannot be emphasised, since it defines the trajectory of the individual's journey through the darkness.

Depression often isolates individuals, causing a sensation of loneliness that can be as devastating as the disorder itself. A helpful companion becomes a lifeline, a source of comfort and understanding in times of distress. Through knowledgeable and empathic care, a loved one can counteract the isolating effects of depression, creating connection and strengthening the individual's sense of belonging.

Furthermore, supporting a loved one through depression is an investment in the relationship itself. It demands a deep pool of patience, as the geography of depression is defined by peaks and valleys. Understanding that the path may be long and tough, yet choosing to stick by a loved one, shows a genuine commitment to the relationship's strength and resilience.

In essence, this book tries to underline the necessity of helping a loved one through depression as a tool not only to lessen their suffering but also to build the links of love and understanding within the relationship. It is a tribute to the conviction that, even in the worst situations, love can be a transformative force, moving individuals and their partners toward healing and hope.

The prevalence of depression is a global reality, affecting individuals and relationships with equal force. This exploration has touched upon the widespread impact of depression and the very personal purpose motivating the production of this guide.

Chapter 1

<u>**UNDERSTANDING DEPRESSION**</u>

At its heart, depression is a multidimensional mental health illness that affects an individual's thoughts, emotions, and behaviours. Defining depression includes comprehending its numerous manifestations, each posing unique challenges for people who deal with its weight.

Major Depressive Disorder (MDD): This is the most recognized kind of depression, characterised by persistent feelings of melancholy, loss of interest or pleasure in activities, changes in eating or sleep patterns, and a lack of energy. MDD can considerably affect daily functioning and typically recurs throughout a person's life.

Persistent Depressive Disorder (PDD): Formerly known as dysthymia, PDD entails chronic, low-grade depression lasting for at least two years. While less severe than MDD, its chronic nature can have a substantial influence on a person's quality of life.

Bipolar Disorder: This disorder comprises cycles of depression and mania. Individuals with bipolar illness experience intense highs (mania) and lows (depression), with periods of normal mood in between. The fluctuations in mood can be severe and bothersome.

Seasonal Affective Disorder (SAD): Linked to changes in seasons, notably during fall and winter when there is less sunlight, SAD leads to depression symptoms such as low energy, irritability, and changes in sleep habits.

Postpartum Depression: Affecting some new moms, postpartum depression involves feelings of severe sadness, worry, and tiredness following childbirth. It can interfere with the ability to care for oneself and the new baby.

Understanding these distinct varieties of depression is vital for identifying the varied ways in which individuals experience and express their challenges. Each kind necessitates a unique approach to support and treatment.

Exploring Common Symptoms and Signs

Recognizing depression includes being alert to a variety of symptoms and indicators that appear in individuals. While each person's experience is unique, many similar symptoms might act as red flags:

1. Persistent Sadness or Hopelessness: Feelings of intense sadness or a sense of

hopelessness that persists over an extended period.

2. Loss of Interest or Pleasure: A lessened interest or pleasure in activities that were once enjoyable, typically leading to social disengagement.

3. Changes in Sleep Patterns: Insomnia or excessive sleeping can be suggestive of depression, altering the natural sleep-wake cycle.

4. Changes in Appetite or Weight: Significant weight loss or increase, coupled with changes in appetite, might be a physical expression of depression feelings.

5. Exhaustion and Lack of Energy: Individuals with depression often have a continuous sense of exhaustion, even after enough rest.

6. Difficulty Concentrating: Cognitive skills may be compromised, leading to difficulties in concentrating, making judgments, or recalling details.

7. Feelings of Guilt or Worthlessness: A skewed self-perception may lead to excessive guilt, feelings of worthlessness, or constant self-criticism.

8. Physical Symptoms: Unexplained aches and pains, headaches, or digestive troubles often accompany depressive illnesses.

Recognizing these indications is a vital step in early intervention and support. It lays the framework for comprehending the depth of an individual's struggle and guides the development of compassionate responses.

Breaking Down Misconceptions and Stigma Surrounding Depression

Despite growing awareness of mental health issues, misunderstandings and stigmas around depression persist, contributing to a culture of silence and isolation. Breaking down these myths is crucial in building a climate of understanding and support.

Misconception 1: Depression is a decision or Sign of Weakness: Depression is not a decision, nor is it indicative of personal weakness. It is a complex interplay of genetic, biochemical, environmental, and psychological elements.

Misconception 2: Happiness Alone will Cure Depression: While pleasant experiences and situations are beneficial, depression typically requires professional assistance, and the naive assumption that sheer happiness will cure it oversimplifies a complicated mental health disease.

Misconception 3: Depression is simply melancholy: Depression transcends beyond typical melancholy. It comprises a variety of emotional, cognitive, and physical symptoms that profoundly disrupt daily living.

Misconception 4: Seeking aid is a show of Failure: Seeking aid is a show of strength and resilience. Professional assistance, whether through therapy, counselling, or medicine, is a proactive step towards recovery.

Misconception 5: Depressed Individuals Are Always Withdrawn: Depression manifests differently in each individual. While some may retreat socially, others may engage in high-functioning depression, disguising their troubles beneath a facade of normalcy.

Addressing these myths produces a more informed and empathetic society, eliminating the obstacles to getting help and establishing an environment where individuals feel validated in their experiences.

<u>The Impact of Depression on Relationships</u>

The ripples of depression stretch far beyond the individual, dramatically altering the dynamics of relationships. Understanding this impact is vital for partners, family members, and friends who find themselves navigating the rough waters alongside their loved one.

1. <u>Communication Challenges:</u> Depression typically impedes effective communication. The individual may struggle to communicate their feelings, and partners may find it tough to understand the intensity of their emotional pain.

2. <u>Emotional Distance:</u> The emotional weight of sadness can generate a sense of

distance between partners. The affected individual may feel emotionally unavailable, and the partner may struggle to bridge the gap.

3. <u>Changes in Intimacy:</u> Depression can dramatically disrupt intimacy, leading to changes in sexual desire, physical closeness, and general connection between couples.

4. <u>Role Reversals:</u> In some circumstances, the partner may take on the role of a caretaker, balancing emotional support with the responsibilities of daily life. This alteration can affect the dynamics of the partnership.

5. <u>Strain on Support Systems:</u> Friends and family members may also experience strain as they endeavour to support the affected individual while regulating their own emotional responses to the circumstance.

Understanding the effects of depression on relationships is the first step in handling these issues effectively. It demands a delicate balance of empathy, patience, and a dedication to promoting open communication.

Understanding depression means unravelling its intricacies, from the varied shapes it might take to the common indications that act as beacons for support. Breaking down myths and deconstructing stigmas around depression promotes a more empathetic environment for people suffering with its weight.

The impact of depression on relationships underlines the linked nature of mental health, underlining the necessity for informed, empathic support systems.

Chapter 2

<u>NAVIGATING THE EMOTIONAL LANDSCAPE</u>

Depression is not merely a mental health problem; it's a profound emotional experience that engulfs folks in a complicated and often stormy terrain. Navigating this emotional rollercoaster demands a deep awareness of the intricacies involved.

<u>Examining the Emotional Rollercoaster of Depression</u>

Depression is sometimes described as a rollercoaster, a metaphor that depicts the unpredictable highs and lows experienced by individuals. Understanding this emotional rollercoaster is fundamental to offering appropriate support.

1. <u>Intense Sadness and Despair:</u> At the root of the rollercoaster is an overwhelming sense of sadness and despair. Individuals with depression typically describe feeling buried in a deep abyss of darkness, where even the simplest activities might feel overwhelming.

2. <u>Apathy and Emotional Numbness:</u> Counteracting the deep melancholy is a pervasive numbness, a detachment from feelings. This emotional numbing can show as apathy, as individuals struggle to find interest or pleasure in activities that once offered joy.

3. <u>Fluctuating Moods:</u> The rollercoaster nature of depression involves unpredictable mood swings. Moments of relative stability may be unexpectedly disturbed by powerful waves of melancholy or irritation.

4. <u>Anxiety and Restlessness:</u> Depression is not simply characterised by sadness; it

typically coexists with anxiety and restlessness. Individuals may have a continual undercurrent of concern and tension.

5. <u>Guilt and Self-Blame:</u> Depression typically brings forth sentiments of guilt and self-blame. Individuals may harbour irrational notions about their worth and engage in constant self-criticism.

6. <u>Lack of Motivation:</u> The rollercoaster of depression often includes times of deep fatigue and a lack of motivation. Even basic chores can become huge undertakings.

Examining this emotional rollercoaster provides insight into the daily problems faced by those with depression. It highlights the necessity for a sympathetic and adaptable support structure that can navigate the peaks and valleys of their emotional environment.

How Depression May Affect Communication and Expression of Emotions

The influence of depression on communication is substantial, changing how individuals express themselves and connect with others.

1. <u>Difficulty Articulating Emotions:</u> Depression can present a barrier to successful communication by making it challenging for individuals to describe their emotions. The intensity and complexity of their inner experiences may defy language expression.

2. <u>Retreat and Isolation: The</u> emotional weight of depression often leads to retreat and isolation. Individuals may hide from social engagements, making it harder for others to grasp the emotional upheaval they are experiencing.

3. <u>Negative Cognitive Patterns:</u> Depression is distinguished by negative thought patterns that can distort perceptions and inhibit effective communication. Individuals may view neutral or positive signals as evidence of their perceived deficiencies.

4. <u>Emotional Flatness:</u> The emotional numbness associated with depression can result in a flat affect, when individuals struggle to portray a range of feelings. This emotional flatness can be mistaken as disinterest or apathy.

5. <u>Concern of Burdening Others:</u> Individuals with depression may hesitate to communicate their emotions owing to a concern of burdening others. This dread can lead to a sense of isolation and intensify the obstacles of reaching out for support.

Understanding these interactions is vital for partners, family members, and friends who strive to help their loved ones. Effective communication entails not just listening to spoken words but also perceiving the unspoken emotional currents behind them.

Strategies for Empathetic Listening and Validating Feelings

Empathetic listening and validating feelings are cornerstones of effective support for someone navigating the emotional landscape of depression. These tactics establish a secure and validating atmosphere, encouraging a sense of connection and understanding.

1. Cultivate Active Listening Skills: Active listening entails fully interacting with the speaker, giving them your whole attention, and responding in a way that displays understanding. Avoid interrupting, and use non-verbal indicators such as nodding to express your attentiveness.

2. <u>Practise Reflective Listening:</u> Reflective listening entails paraphrasing and summarising what the individual has communicated to assure understanding. This not only demonstrates that you are actively listening but also allows for clarification and validation.

3. <u>Avoid Judgment and Assumptions:</u> Create a non-judgmental atmosphere where individuals feel free to express their emotions without fear of censure. Avoid making assumptions or delivering unwanted advice; instead, focus on acknowledging their experiences.

4. <u>Validate Emotions without reducing:</u> Validating sentiments involves accepting the legitimacy of the individual's emotions without reducing or disregarding them. Phrases such as "I hear you," or "It's okay to feel that way" express empathy and compassion.

5. <u>Use Open-Ended Questions:</u> Encourage open communication by asking open-ended questions that enable folks to share more about their experiences. This can let them express their emotions more openly.

6. <u>Be Mindful of Body Language:</u> Pay attention to both verbal and non-verbal messages. Sometimes, emotions are transmitted through body language, facial expressions, or gestures. Sensitivity to these clues boosts your ability to understand the emotional context.

7. <u>Offer Support, Not answers:</u> While the temptation to suggest answers is normal, individuals with depression frequently need support more than advice. Let them know you are there for them and eager to help them in whatever way they need.

Empathetic listening and validating sentiments develop a foundation of trust and understanding. These tactics not only assist in navigating the emotional rollercoaster but also contribute to the individual's overall sense of being heard and valued.

Understanding and managing the emotional landscape of depression demands a comprehensive approach that goes beyond surface-level understanding. By exploring the emotional rollercoaster, recognizing the influence on communication, and practising skills for empathic listening, we lay the framework for effective assistance.

Chapter 3

<u>BUILDING A SUPPORTIVE FOUNDATION</u>

Depression casts a long shadow, affecting not just the individual who grapples with its intricacies but also others who stand by them.

In this inquiry, we delve into the crucial responsibility of developing a supportive foundation for partners of persons navigating the path of depression.

From understanding the pivotal role of a supportive partner to establishing open communication, setting realistic expectations, and fostering a sense of safety and trust, this guide aims to provide insights and strategies for creating a resilient and compassionate relationship in the face of mental health challenges.

<u>The Role of a Supportive Partner in the Journey through Depression</u>

The role of a supporting spouse in the road through depression is multidimensional, needing a careful mix of understanding, empathy, and unshakable dedication.

1. <u>Be a Compassionate Listener:</u> The simple act of listening with empathy can be transforming. Allow your spouse to communicate their feelings without judgement or interference. Sometimes, the act of verbalising their emotions can be a critical step in the healing process.

2. <u>Educate Yourself about Depression:</u> Understanding the subtleties of depression is key. Educate yourself on the symptoms, treatments, and potential obstacles. This information empowers you to provide informed support and decreases the probability of misconceptions.

3. <u>Be Patient and Understanding:</u> Patience is a virtue while assisting a partner through depression. The journey is typically nonlinear, defined by progress and failures. Approach each day with understanding, acknowledging that healing is a slow process.

4. <u>Encourage Professional Help:</u> While your support is vital, depression often requires professional help. Encourage your partner to seek treatment or counselling, and if needed, accompany them to appointments. Collaborate with mental health providers to establish a comprehensive support system.

5. <u>Share the Burden:</u> Depression may be isolating, and individuals may feel burdened by their troubles. Share the emotional strain by expressing your commitment to enduring the storm together. Reinforce that they are not alone in overcoming the obstacles that lie ahead.

6. <u>Celebrate Small Victories:</u> Recognize and celebrate even the smallest victories. Whether it's getting out of bed, attending a therapy session, or engaging in a previously enjoyed activity, acknowledging these achievements fosters a positive environment.

The role of a supportive partner is not about "fixing" the individual but rather providing a steady presence and unwavering support as they navigate the complexities of their mental health journey.

Establishing Open and Honest Communication

Communication serves as the backbone of any healthy relationship, and when faced with the problems of depression, open and honest communication becomes even more vital.

1. <u>Create a Safe Space:</u> Establish an environment where open conversation is accepted and valued. Ensure that your partner feels safe expressing their thoughts and emotions without fear of judgement.

2. <u>Use "I" sentences:</u> Frame your thoughts and sentiments using "I" sentences to avoid putting blame. For example, say, "I feel concerned when I see you withdrawing," rather than, "You always isolate yourself."

3. <u>Be Mindful of Timing:</u> Choose acceptable moments to initiate conversations about difficult issues. Avoid discussing difficult things during moments of heightened emotional discomfort, and instead, select calm and quiet moments for meaningful dialogue.

4. <u>Practise Active Listening:</u> Actively listen to your partner's words, but also pay attention to their non-verbal signs. Reflect back what you hear to ensure understanding

and indicate that you are fully engaged in the conversation.

5. <u>Encourage Emotional Expression:</u> Allow and encourage your spouse to express their emotions openly. Create a space where they feel comfortable sharing both positive and negative feelings without judgement.

6. <u>Validate Emotions:</u> Validating your partner's emotions is crucial. Let them know that their sentiments are acknowledged and appreciated, even if you may not fully understand. This confirmation develops a sense of being heard and understood.

Open and honest communication develops a foundation of trust and transparency. It serves as a bridge between partners, allowing them to navigate the challenges of depression with a shared understanding.

<u>Setting Realistic Expectations and Boundaries</u>

Navigating depression requires a realistic approach to expectations and the establishment of healthy boundaries within the relationship.

1. <u>Realistic Expectations for Progress:</u> Understand that progress may be slow and nonlinear. Set realistic expectations for the pace of recovery, knowing that healing is a gradual process with both ups and downs.

2. <u>Communicate About Needs and Limitations:</u> Engage in open conversations about each other's needs and limitations. Discuss what support looks like for both partners and establish boundaries that protect the well-being of both individuals.

3. <u>Foster Independence:</u> While offering support, encourage your partner's independence. Allow them the agency to make decisions about their treatment and

involve them in talks about the support they find most valuable.

4. <u>Establish Self-Care Practices:</u> Both partners need to emphasise self-care. Establish self-care practices individually and as a pair. This may involve setting aside time for personal interests, exercise, or leisure to recharge emotional batteries.

5. <u>Be Flexible:</u> Flexibility is crucial in handling the obstacles of depression. Plans may need to be changed, and unforeseen setbacks may arise. A flexible attitude enables for adaptability in the face of the unpredictable nature of depression.

6. <u>Seek Professional help:</u> If needed, seek professional help to create healthy limits and expectations. A therapist or counsellor can provide insights and solutions for managing the intricacies of a relationship damaged by depression.

Setting realistic expectations and limitations is not about reducing standards but about providing a framework that respects the specific challenges provided by depression and provides an environment favourable to growth and healing.

Fostering a Sense of Safety and Trust

In the area of depression, building a sense of safety and trust is paramount. These characteristics establish a foundation upon which a durable and supportive relationship can be created.

1. Non-Judgmental Support: Offer support without judgement. Create a setting where your spouse feels safe expressing their thoughts and emotions, knowing that they will be met with understanding and compassion.

2. Consistent Reliability: Be a consistent and reliable presence in your partner's life. Reliability promotes a sense of security,

reminding your partner that they can count on you, even in the midst of the emotional problems offered by depression.

3. <u>Confidentiality and Privacy:</u> Respect your partner's privacy and maintain confidentiality about their experiences with depression. Trust is built when individuals feel confidence that their vulnerabilities are handled with sensitivity.

4. <u>Transparent Communication:</u> Practise transparent communication. Share your views and feelings openly, and encourage your spouse to do the same. Transparency promotes confidence and reinforces the feeling that both individuals are working jointly towards a shared understanding.

5. <u>Collaborative Decision-Making:</u> Involve your spouse in decision-making processes relating to their mental health. Collaborative decision-making empowers individuals to

take an active role in their treatment and reinforces trust in the relationship.

6.   Express   Unconditional   Love: Communicate your love and dedication unconditionally. Let your partner know that your support is not contingent upon their ability to "overcome" depression but is rooted in a genuine desire to be there for them through thick and thin.

Fostering a sense of safety and trust requires intentional efforts to create a space where vulnerability is welcomed, and individuals can feel secure in the knowledge that they are not alone in their struggles.

Building a supportive foundation in the context of depression is a multifaceted endeavour that involves recognizing the pivotal role of a supportive partner, establishing   open   and   honest communication,   setting   realistic expectations and boundaries, and fostering a sense of safety and trust.

As we progress through this book, the subsequent chapters will explore practical strategies for daily life, seeking professional help, addressing challenges in intimacy, and celebrating progress and resilience. By integrating these insights and strategies, partners can navigate the complexities of loving someone with depression with empathy, resilience, and a strengthened bond.

Chapter 4

<u>PRACTICAL STRATEGIES FOR DAILY LIFE</u>

Daily life, often consisting of routine and responsibilities, takes on a unique complexity when one is navigating the challenges of depression.

In this exploration, we will delve into practical strategies that can be woven into the fabric of daily existence to support mental health.

From the establishment of a routine that fosters stability to the encouragement of self-care practices, addressing challenges related to sleep, nutrition, and exercise, and finding the delicate balance between responsibilities and limitations, these strategies aim to provide a roadmap for individuals and their partners on the journey through depression.

Creating a Routine that Supports Mental Health

A well-structured routine serves as a stabilising force, offering predictability and a sense of order that can be particularly beneficial for individuals grappling with depression.

1. <u>Set Consistent Daily Goals:</u> Establish realistic and attainable goals for each day. These goals can be small, such as getting out of bed at a specific time, completing a household task, or engaging in a hobby. Consistent achievement of daily goals contributes to a sense of accomplishment.

2. <u>Prioritise Sleep:</u> Establish a consistent sleep schedule. Adequate and quality sleep is crucial for mental health, and irregular sleep patterns can exacerbate the symptoms

of depression. Create a bedtime routine that promotes relaxation and signals to the body that it is time to wind down.

3. <u>Incorporate Mindfulness Practices:</u> Integrate mindfulness practices into your daily routine. Whether it's meditation, deep breathing exercises, or simply taking a few moments to be present in the current moment, mindfulness can help manage stress and anxiety.

4. <u>Plan Enjoyable Activities:</u> Schedule activities that bring joy and pleasure. These could be social interactions, hobbies, or activities that have historically brought a sense of fulfilment. Incorporating enjoyable activities into the routine contributes to a positive outlook.

5. <u>Break Tasks into Manageable Steps:</u> When faced with larger tasks, break them down into smaller, more manageable steps. This approach makes tasks less

overwhelming and allows for a sense of accomplishment with each completed step.

6. <u>Create a Balanced Schedule:</u> Strive for a balance between work, leisure, and self-care activities. Avoid overloading the schedule with responsibilities, and allocate time for rest and relaxation.

Creating a routine that supports mental health requires a thoughtful and adaptable approach. The goal is not rigidity but rather a flexible structure that fosters stability and well-being.

Encouraging Self-Care and Healthy Habits

Self-care is a cornerstone of mental health, and its importance is magnified when navigating the challenges of depression. Encouraging healthy habits contributes to a holistic approach to well-being.

1. <u>Establish a Self-Care Routine:</u> Develop a consistent self-care routine that encompasses activities that promote mental, emotional, and physical well-being. This may include practices such as journaling, taking a warm bath, or engaging in creative pursuits.

2. <u>Prioritise Nutrition:</u> Pay attention to nutritional choices. Aim for a balanced diet that includes a variety of fruits, vegetables, whole grains, and lean proteins. Nutrient-rich foods can positively impact mood and energy levels.

3. <u>Hydration:</u> Staying hydrated is a simple yet often overlooked aspect of self-care. Dehydration can contribute to fatigue and impact cognitive function. Make a conscious effort to drink an adequate amount of water throughout the day.

4. <u>Establish Healthy Sleep Hygiene:</u> In addition to setting a consistent sleep

schedule, practise good sleep hygiene. This includes creating a comfortable sleep environment, limiting screen time before bedtime, and avoiding stimulants like caffeine in the evening.

5. <u>Engage in Physical Activity:</u> Exercise has been shown to have a positive impact on mood and can be a powerful tool in managing depression. Incorporate physical activity into your routine, even if it's a short walk or gentle stretching exercises.

6. <u>Connect with Nature:</u> Spending time outdoors and connecting with nature can have therapeutic effects on mental health. Whether it's a walk in the park, gardening, or simply sitting in a natural setting, nature has a calming influence.

Encouraging self-care and healthy habits is not a luxury but a fundamental aspect of maintaining mental health. These practices contribute to resilience and provide individuals with the tools to navigate the challenges of daily life.

Addressing Challenges Such as Sleep, Nutrition, and Exercise

Challenges related to sleep, nutrition, and exercise can significantly impact mental health, especially for individuals dealing with depression. Addressing these challenges requires a comprehensive and individualised approach.

1. Sleep Challenges:

- Identify and address factors contributing to sleep disturbances, such as excessive screen time, irregular sleep patterns, or an uncomfortable sleep environment.
- Establish a calming bedtime routine to signal to the body that it is time to wind down.
- Consider consulting a healthcare professional if sleep challenges persist. They can provide guidance on potential

underlying issues and recommend strategies for improvement.

2. Nutrition Challenges:
- Aim for a balanced and varied diet that includes a mix of fruits, vegetables, whole grains, lean proteins, and healthy fats.
- Be mindful of emotional eating patterns. Recognize when emotions may be influencing eating habits and seek alternative coping mechanisms.
- Consult with a registered dietitian or nutritionist for personalised guidance on nutrition and dietary choices.

3. Exercise Challenges:
- Start with small, achievable physical activities and gradually increase intensity and duration.
- Choose activities that are enjoyable to make exercise a positive and sustainable part of the routine.

- Explore different forms of exercise, such as walking, yoga, or dancing, to find what suits individual preferences.

Addressing these challenges involves a gradual and compassionate approach. Small, sustainable changes in sleep, nutrition, and exercise habits can collectively contribute to improved mental health.

Balancing Responsibilities and Understanding Limitations

Balancing responsibilities becomes a delicate task when managing depression. Understanding and acknowledging limitations is key to creating a sustainable and supportive environment.

1. Prioritise Essential Tasks: Identify and prioritise essential tasks while recognizing that not everything needs to be accomplished in a single day. Focus on the

most critical responsibilities and break them down into manageable steps.

2. <u>Communicate with Others:</u> Open communication with partners, family members, or colleagues about current challenges and limitations. Setting realistic expectations with others fosters understanding and reduces unnecessary stress.

3. <u>Learn to Delegate:</u> Recognize the power of delegation. It's okay to ask for help and share responsibilities with others. Delegating tasks can alleviate some of the pressure and create space for self-care.

4. <u>Set Boundaries:</u> Establish clear boundaries to protect mental and emotional well-being. This may involve setting limits on work hours, avoiding overcommitment, and saying no when necessary. Boundaries are a form of self-care.

5. <u>Break Tasks into Manageable Steps:</u> Large tasks can be overwhelming, leading to a sense of paralysis. Break tasks into smaller, more manageable steps, and celebrate achievements along the way.

6. <u>Practice Self-Compassion:</u> Be kind to yourself. Understand that there will be days when productivity is lower, and that's okay. Practising self-compassion involves treating oneself with the same kindness and understanding offered to others.

Balancing responsibilities requires a constant reassessment of priorities and a willingness to adapt. By understanding limitations and embracing self-compassion, individuals can navigate daily life with greater resilience and self-awareness.

Practical strategies for daily life form the bedrock of mental health support for individuals dealing with depression. From creating a routine that fosters stability to encouraging self-care and healthy habits, addressing challenges related to sleep, nutrition, and exercise, and finding the delicate balance between responsibilities and limitations, these strategies contribute to a holistic approach to well-being.

Chapter 5

SEEKING PROFESSIONAL HELP

In the intricate landscape of depression, seeking professional help is a pivotal step towards understanding, managing, and overcoming the challenges it presents.

By embracing these aspects of seeking professional help, individuals and their partners can navigate the complexities of depression with a comprehensive and supportive approach.

The Importance of Professional Intervention

Depression is a multifaceted mental health condition that often requires specialised knowledge and support for effective management. Professional intervention plays a crucial role in addressing the complexities of depression for several reasons.

1. <u>Expert Assessment and Diagnosis:</u> Mental health professionals, including psychologists, psychiatrists, and therapists, possess the expertise to assess and diagnose depression accurately. Their training equips them to recognize the nuances of different depressive disorders and tailor interventions accordingly.

2. <u>Tailored Treatment Plans:</u> Professionals can develop personalised treatment plans based on the individual's unique needs and circumstances. This may include a combination of therapeutic modalities, medication, and lifestyle adjustments.

3. <u>Access to Evidence-Based Therapies:</u> Therapies such as Cognitive-Behavioral Therapy (CBT), Dialectical Behavior Therapy (DBT), and Mindfulness-Based Cognitive Therapy (MBCT) have

demonstrated efficacy in treating depression. Professional intervention provides access to these evidence-based therapies.

4. <u>Monitoring Progress:</u> Regular sessions with a mental health professional allow for the ongoing monitoring of progress. Adjustments to the treatment plan can be made as needed, ensuring that interventions remain effective throughout the journey.

5. <u>Crisis Intervention:</u> In moments of crisis or heightened distress, professionals are equipped to provide immediate support and intervention. This can be crucial in preventing and managing acute episodes of depression.

6. <u>Holistic Approach:</u> Mental health professionals adopt a holistic approach to treatment, considering not only the symptoms of depression but also the

individual's overall well-being, relationships, and life circumstances.

7. <u>Validation and Empathy:</u> Professionals offer a safe and non-judgmental space for individuals to express their thoughts and emotions. Validation and empathy are integral components of the therapeutic relationship, fostering a sense of understanding and support.

Engaging with mental health professionals provides individuals with a structured and informed approach to managing depression. It empowers them to navigate the complexities of their mental health journey with guidance and support.

Encouraging and Supporting Therapy or Counselling

Embracing therapy or counselling is a significant and transformative step in the journey through depression. Encouraging and supporting a loved one in seeking therapeutic intervention involves fostering an environment of understanding and dismantling potential barriers.

1. <u>Normalise the Process:</u> Destigmatize therapy by normalising the idea of seeking professional help. Emphasise that therapy is a proactive and courageous step towards self-improvement and mental well-being.

2. <u>Communicate Openly:</u> Initiate open and non-judgmental conversations about therapy. Encourage your partner to share their thoughts, concerns, and expectations about the therapeutic process. Active listening fosters a sense of being heard and understood.

3. <u>Highlight the Benefits:</u> Discuss the potential benefits of therapy, emphasising its role in developing coping strategies, improving emotional well-being, and fostering personal growth. Share success stories or testimonials if appropriate.

4. <u>Offer to Explore Options Together:</u> Research and explore therapy options together. This collaborative approach communicates your commitment to supporting the process. Help identify therapists or counselling approaches that align with your partner's preferences and needs.

5. <u>Attend Sessions Together:</u> In some cases, attending therapy sessions together can be beneficial. This not only provides support to the individual seeking therapy but also allows partners to gain insights, improve communication, and strengthen the overall therapeutic process.

6. <u>Respect Autonomy:</u> While encouragement is essential, respect your partner's autonomy in the decision to pursue therapy. Pressuring or coercing someone into therapy may create resistance and hinder the therapeutic relationship.

7. <u>Celebrate Progress:</u> Acknowledge and celebrate milestones and progress made during therapy. Recognizing the positive impact of therapy reinforces the idea that seeking professional help is a worthwhile and empowering endeavour.

Encouraging and supporting therapy requires a collaborative and empathetic approach. By fostering an open and understanding environment, partners can play a vital role in making therapy a positive and transformative experience.

Understanding Medication and Its Role in Treatment

Medication can be an integral component of depression treatment, often prescribed in conjunction with therapy. Understanding the role of medication, its benefits, potential side effects, and considerations is crucial for informed decision-making.

1.   Addressing   Chemical   Imbalances:
Depression   is   often   associated   with
imbalances in neurotransmitters, the brain's
chemical messengers. Medications, such as
antidepressants, aim to restore balance by
influencing   the   levels   of   these
neurotransmitters.

2. Enhancing the Effectiveness of Therapy:
Medication can enhance the effectiveness of
therapy. By   alleviating   some   of   the
physiological   symptoms   of   depression,
individuals may be better able to engage in
therapeutic   processes,   such   as   cognitive
restructuring or behaviour modification.

3.   Managing   Severe   Symptoms: For
individuals experiencing severe symptoms
of depression, medication may provide more
immediate   relief.   It   can   be   a   crucial
intervention   in   stabilising   mood   and
preventing further deterioration of mental
health.

4. <u>Individualised Treatment Plans:</u> Mental health professionals tailor treatment plans to the individual's needs. The decision to prescribe medication is made based on factors such as the severity of symptoms, response to previous treatments, and the presence of co-occurring conditions.

5. <u>Potential Side Effects:</u> Medications may have side effects, which can vary from person to person. It's important to discuss potential side effects with a healthcare provider and weigh the benefits against the risks. Regular monitoring helps manage side effects effectively.

6. <u>Collaborative Decision-Making:</u> The decision to include medication in the treatment plan is a collaborative one. Healthcare providers engage in open discussions with individuals, addressing their concerns and preferences. Informed consent is a crucial aspect of the decision-making process.

7. <u>Gradual Adjustment and Monitoring:</u> Medications are often introduced gradually, allowing for careful monitoring of their effects. Adjustments may be made based on an individual's response and any emerging side effects. Regular check-ins with healthcare providers ensure ongoing assessment and optimization of treatment.

Understanding medication involves active participation in the decision-making process. It's a dynamic aspect of depression treatment that should be approached with collaboration, transparency, and a commitment to ongoing monitoring.

The Collaborative Role of Partners in the Therapeutic Process

Partners play a significant and collaborative role in supporting the therapeutic journey. This involvement contributes to the overall effectiveness of the therapeutic process and enhances the well-being of both individuals.

1. <u>Attend Sessions Together:</u> In certain cases, attending therapy sessions together can be beneficial. This collaborative approach provides partners with insights into the therapeutic process, facilitates open communication, and fosters a shared understanding of the challenges being addressed.

2. <u>Foster a Supportive Environment:</u> Create a supportive environment at home that complements the therapeutic work. Encourage open communication, active listening, and the application of therapeutic insights in daily life. A home environment that aligns with therapeutic goals reinforces positive changes.

3. <u>Implement Therapeutic Strategies:</u> Partners can actively participate in implementing therapeutic strategies recommended by the therapist. This may involve practising communication skills,

engaging in joint activities that promote connection, and collaborating on coping strategies.

4. <u>Respect Therapeutic Confidentiality</u>: Respect the confidentiality of the therapeutic relationship. While collaboration is essential, certain aspects of the therapeutic process are confidential. Discuss boundaries with the therapist and your partner to ensure a balance between support and privacy.

5. <u>Provide Emotional Support</u>: Emotional support is a fundamental aspect of the collaborative role of partners. Acknowledge the challenges faced by your loved one, express empathy, and offer reassurance. Your consistent presence and understanding contribute to a sense of security.

6. <u>Encourage Consistency</u>: Consistency is key in supporting the therapeutic process. Encourage your partner to attend therapy

sessions regularly and engage consistently in therapeutic activities. This dedication enhances the effectiveness of therapeutic interventions.

7. <u>Share Observations and Perspectives:</u> Partners can offer valuable insights by sharing their observations and perspectives. Communicate openly about positive changes, challenges, and areas where additional support may be beneficial. This collaborative dialogue strengthens the therapeutic alliance.

Partners are integral allies in the therapeutic journey. By actively participating in the process, offering support, and fostering a collaborative approach, they contribute to the overall success of the therapeutic intervention and the well-being of their loved ones.

Seeking professional help is a transformative and essential step in the journey through depression. The importance of professional intervention cannot be overstated, as it brings expert assessment, tailored treatment plans, access to evidence-based therapies, and ongoing support.

Encouraging and supporting therapy or counselling involves normalising the process, communicating openly, and fostering a collaborative approach. Understanding medication and its role in treatment requires informed decision-making, consideration of potential side effects, and ongoing monitoring.

The collaborative role of partners in the therapeutic process is multifaceted, involving active participation, emotional support, and a commitment to creating a supportive home environment.

Chapter 6

ADDRESSING CHALLENGES IN INTIMACY

Intimacy, a cornerstone of romantic relationships, can be profoundly affected by the shadows of depression. By navigating these complexities with empathy and resilience, individuals and their partners can foster a deeper understanding and connection within the realm of intimacy.

The Impact of Depression on Intimacy and Sexual Health

Depression casts a wide-reaching shadow that extends into various aspects of an individual's life, including their capacity for intimacy and sexual health. Understanding the impact of depression on these domains is crucial for navigating challenges within a relationship.

1. <u>Changes in Libido:</u> One of the most common effects of depression on intimacy is a shift in libido. Individuals may experience a decrease in sexual desire, leading to a potential misalignment in the sexual dynamics of the relationship.

2. <u>Emotional Distance:</u> Depression can create emotional distance between partners. Feelings of sadness, apathy, and disconnection may permeate the emotional landscape, hindering the ability to connect intimately.

3. <u>Negative Body Image:</u> Depression often influences how individuals perceive themselves, leading to negative body image issues. This can contribute to feelings of self-consciousness and impact one's comfort and confidence in intimate situations.

4. <u>Fatigue and Lethargy:</u> The pervasive fatigue and lethargy associated with depression can affect energy levels and,

consequently, the motivation and ability to engage in intimate activities.

5. <u>Difficulty Communicating Needs:</u> Depression can make it challenging for individuals to communicate their needs, desires, and boundaries regarding intimacy. A lack of communication can lead to misunderstandings and increased tension in the relationship.

6. <u>Impact on Relationship Satisfaction:</u> The cumulative effect of these factors can contribute to a decline in overall relationship satisfaction. Intimacy is a fundamental component of romantic relationships, and when impaired, it can strain the emotional connection between couples.

Understanding the influence of depression on intimacy needs a sophisticated grasp of the physical, emotional, and psychological components at play. By understanding these challenges, individuals and their partners can begin to work jointly towards sustaining a good connection.

Communicating About Intimacy with Sensitivity and Understanding

Communication is the key in addressing issues in intimacy among depression. Approaching these interactions with sensitivity and empathy is vital for developing open discourse and connection.

1. Choose the Right Time and place: Initiate conversations about intimacy in a comfortable and private place. Choose a time when both parties are calm and receptive to discussions, avoiding situations of heightened stress or anxiety.

2. Use "I" Statements: Frame discussions using "I" statements to describe feelings and experiences without assigning blame. For example, say, "I've been feeling a bit distant lately, and I wanted to talk about how we

can reconnect," rather than, "You never initiate intimacy anymore."

3. <u>Express Empathy and Understanding:</u> Acknowledge the impact of depression on both partners and express empathy. Understanding that depression affects individuals differently allows for a more empathetic and collaborative approach to problem-solving.

4. <u>Avoid Judgement:</u> Steer clear of judgement or criticism. Instead, approach the conversation with a genuine willingness to understand each other's perspectives and develop answers collaboratively.

5. <u>Encourage Active Listening:</u> Actively listen to your partner's thoughts and feelings without interruption. Reflect back what you hear to assure understanding and validate their experiences. Active listening develops a sense of being heard and respected.

6. <u>Be Patient:</u> Recognize that these conversations may require time and patience. Be patient with the process and avoid pressing your partner to open up or make fast changes. Building comprehension is a gradual journey.

7. <u>Collaborate on Solutions:</u> Approach the conversation as a collaborative effort to identify solutions. Discuss various tactics for preserving closeness, and be open to attempting new approaches that respond to both partners' needs and comfort levels.

Sensitivity and understanding constitute the cornerstone of good communication regarding intimacy among depression. By building an environment of transparency and mutual support, partners may negotiate difficult conversations with empathy and resilience.

Strategies for Maintaining a Healthy Connection in the Face of Challenges

Maintaining a healthy connection in the face of adversity demands purposeful efforts and a commitment to maintaining intimacy despite the impact of sadness. The following ideas offer information on how to handle these problems and develop a resilient connection.

1. Prioritise Emotional Connection: While physical closeness is crucial, emphasising emotional connection builds the framework for a strong and successful relationship. Engage in activities that foster emotional bonding, such as common hobbies, meaningful talks, and quality time together.

2. Explore Non-Sexual Intimacy: Intimacy extends beyond sexual activity. Explore non-sexual forms of intimacy, such as hugging, holding hands, or spending time together in ways that encourage emotional

closeness. These forms of connection can be as gratifying.

3. <u>Establish Open Communication:</u> Maintain open communication about feelings, desires, and concerns connected to intimacy. Regular check-ins provide opportunity to address developing needs and agree on tactics for sustaining a good connection.

4. <u>Seek Professional help:</u> Consider obtaining help from a sex therapist or couples counsellor. These professionals specialise in resolving issues related to intimacy and can provide specialised solutions and insights to handle challenges.

5. <u>Schedule Intimate Moments:</u> In the middle of hectic lifestyles and the burden of depression, scheduling intimate moments may be useful. This strategy guarantees that both spouses are aware of and prepared for

these linkages, decreasing stress and ambiguity.

6. <u>Focus on Mutual Pleasure:</u> Shift the focus from performance-based expectations to mutual pleasure. Emphasise the importance of shared experiences that bring joy and fulfilment, rather than assessing success exclusively based on typical concepts of sexual activity.

7. <u>Experiment with Sensuality:</u> Explore sensuality and pleasure in ways that correspond with both partners' comfort levels. This may involve attempting new activities, incorporating sensory experiences, or experimenting with different forms of contact that encourage connection.

8. <u>Support Each Other's Self-Care:</u> Encourage and support each other's self-care routines. Prioritising individual well-being adds to a healthy overall dynamic and offers a basis for intimacy to thrive.

9. <u>Celebrate tiny successes:</u> Acknowledge and celebrate tiny successes in the process towards preserving intimacy. Whether it's having a talk about feelings or adopting a new method, recognizing progress promotes positive efforts.

10. <u>Be Patient and Compassionate:</u> Patience and compassion are essential virtues in navigating challenges in intimacy. Understand that development may be sluggish, and setbacks are a natural part of the process. Approach the process with a mindset of growth and learning.

Maintaining a healthy relationship in the midst of adversities demands ingenuity, adaptation, and a common commitment to nurturing intimacy. By accepting these tactics, individuals and their partners can manage the intricacies of intimacy within depression with resilience and compassion.

Addressing issues in intimacy within the shadows of depression is a sensitive and complicated path. The influence of depression on libido, emotional connection, body image, and communication demands thoughtful attention and joint efforts. Communicating about intimacy with care and empathy is vital for developing open communication and connection.

Strategies for maintaining a healthy relationship involve prioritising emotional bonding, exploring non-sexual forms of intimacy, establishing open communication, obtaining professional help when needed, and having an attitude of patience and compassion.

Chapter 7

<u>WHEN YOUR CHILD IS DEPRESSED</u>

Discovering that your child is battling depression can be a tough and unpleasant realisation. As a parent, it's natural to feel a range of emotions, including concern, perplexity, and a profound desire to help.

This thorough guide seeks to provide insights into understanding childhood depression, detecting signs and symptoms, addressing conversations with compassion, getting professional help, and establishing a supportive environment.

By navigating this road with understanding and sensitivity, parents can play a significant part in their child's path to healing and well-being.

<u>**Understanding Childhood Depression**</u>

Childhood depression is a complicated and varied mental health disease that can impair all elements of a child's life, including their emotions, behaviours, and relationships. Understanding the intricacies of childhood depression is vital for offering appropriate care.

1. Recognizing Signs and Symptoms:

- Persistent Sadness or irritation: Children with depression may exhibit persistent episodes of sadness or irritation that go beyond ordinary mood fluctuations.
- Changes in Sleep Patterns: Depression can disrupt sleep, leading to either insomnia or increased demand for sleep.
- Changes in hunger: Significant changes in hunger, resulting in weight loss or gain, may be suggestive of underlying emotional discomfort.
- Exhaustion and Lack of Energy: A pervasive sense of exhaustion and low

energy levels may influence a child's ability to engage in daily activities.

- Social Withdrawal: Children with depression may retreat from social activities, choosing seclusion over interactions with peers.

- Fall in Academic Performance: Depression can appear in a fall in academic performance, as concentration and motivation may be hampered.

- sentiments of Guilt or Worthlessness: Children may exhibit sentiments of guilt, worthlessness, or self-blame.

- bodily problems: Some children may show depression through bodily problems, such as headaches or stomach aches, without an evident medical explanation.

2. Understanding the Developmental Aspect:

- Childhood depression may appear differently at different developmental stages. Younger children could show their pain through changes in behaviour or play, whereas teenagers may verbalise their emotions more verbally.

- Developmental characteristics, such as cognitive and emotional maturity, influence how children experience and exhibit depression.

3. Differentiating from Normal Emotional States:

- It's vital to discern between normal emotional states and indicators of depression. Children may feel occasional melancholy or anger, but depression involves chronic and pervasive emotional changes that disrupt daily functioning.

4. Risk Factors and Triggers:

- Understanding potential risk factors, such as a family history of depression, exposure to trauma, or chronic stress, can provide insights into the context of a child's emotional well-being.

- Identifying potential triggers, such as academic pressures, social obstacles, or big life changes, might aid in treating underlying stressors.

<u>Approaching Conversations with Sensitivity</u>

Initiating conversations with a youngster about their feelings takes a cautious and supportive approach. Creating an environment where people feel safe expressing their feelings is vital.

1. Choose the Right Time and Setting:

- Select a time and setting where the child feels comfortable and secure. A secluded and peaceful setting can enable an open and honest discourse.

2. Use Open-ended Questions:

- Encourage the child to share their feelings by using open-ended questions. Instead of asking, "Are you sad?" try, "Can you tell me about how you've been feeling lately?"

3. Validate Their Emotions:

- Express empathy and validate their emotions. Let them know that it's alright to feel a range of emotions and that you are there to assist them.

4. Avoid Judgment:

- Refrain from passing judgement or making assumptions. Children need to feel safe expressing their feelings without fear of criticism or blame.

5. Listen Actively:

- Actively listen to what the child is saying. Pay attention to both verbal and non-verbal cues. Reflecting back their emotions can convey that you understand and value their perspective.

6. Reassure Them of Your Support:

- Reassure the child that you are there for them and that seeking help is a sign of strength. Emphasise that they are not alone in their struggles.

7. Be Patient:
- Recognize that the child may need time to open up. Be patient and create an ongoing dialogue where they feel comfortable sharing their experiences.

Approaching conversations with sensitivity fosters trust and communication. It lays the foundation for a supportive relationship where the child feels understood and valued.

Seeking Professional Help
While parental support is crucial, professional intervention is often necessary for addressing childhood depression effectively. Knowing when and how to seek professional help is a vital aspect of providing comprehensive support.

1. Recognizing the Limitations of Parental Support:
- Parents play a significant role in supporting their child's mental health, but

there are limitations to what can be addressed solely through familial support. Professional expertise is essential for comprehensive assessment and intervention.

2. Consulting with a Paediatrician or Family Doctor:

- Begin by consulting with the child's paediatrician or family doctor. These professionals can conduct initial assessments, rule out any underlying medical issues, and provide referrals to mental health specialists.

3. Involving Mental Health Professionals:

- Mental health professionals, such as child psychologists, psychiatrists, or licensed therapists, specialise in assessing and treating childhood depression. They use evidence-based therapeutic approaches to address emotional and behavioural challenges.

4. Considering the Role of School Counsellors:

- School counsellors can be valuable allies in supporting a child's mental health. They can provide insights into the child's academic and social environment and collaborate with mental health professionals for a holistic approach.

5. Exploring Therapy Options:

- Various therapeutic modalities, including Cognitive-Behavioral Therapy (CBT), Play Therapy, and Family Therapy, may be recommended based on the child's age, developmental stage, and specific needs.

6. Evaluating the Need for Medication:

- In some cases, medication may be considered as part of the treatment plan. A child psychiatrist can assess whether medication is appropriate and provide guidance on its use.

7. Engaging in Collaborative Treatment Planning:
- Collaborate with mental health professionals in developing a comprehensive treatment plan. This plan may include therapeutic interventions, coping strategies, and ongoing support for both the child and the family.

Seeking professional help is a proactive and essential step in addressing childhood depression. Professionals bring specialised knowledge and interventions that complement parental support.

<u>Fostering a Supportive Environment at Home</u>

Creating a supportive environment at home is a continuous and integral aspect of helping a child navigate depression. The home environment significantly influences a child's emotional well-being.

1. Encouraging Open Communication:
- Maintain open lines of communication where the child feels comfortable expressing their feelings. Foster an environment where discussions about emotions are met with understanding and empathy.

2. Establishing Routine and Structure:
- Create a stable routine and structure at home. Predictability can provide a sense of security for the child and contribute to overall emotional well-being.

3. Promoting Healthy Lifestyle Habits:
- Encourage healthy lifestyle practices, including frequent exercise, balanced nutrition, and appropriate sleep. Physical well-being is closely linked to emotional well-being.

4. Engaging in Positive Activities:

- Incorporate constructive and fun activities into daily life. Engaging in things the child enjoys can create a sense of accomplishment and delight.

5. Involving the Entire Family:

- Involve the entire family in creating a supportive environment. Siblings and other family members can contribute to a sense of belonging and connection.

6. Modelling Healthy Coping Strategies:

- Model good coping skills for handling stress and emotions. Children often learn by observing, and seeing positive coping mechanisms can be empowering.

7. Collaborating with School and Community Support:

- Collaborate with school and community resources to create a network of support. This may involve communicating with teachers, school counsellors, and community organisations to ensure a holistic approach to the child's well-being.

8. Celebrating Progress:

- Acknowledge and celebrate small victories and progress in the child's journey. Positive reinforcement fosters a sense of accomplishment and reinforces the importance of seeking help.

Fostering a supportive environment involves a collective effort from family, school, and community. By creating a nurturing space, parents contribute significantly to a child's emotional resilience and recovery.

Navigating the issues of childhood depression demands a diverse and caring approach. Understanding the indications and symptoms, conducting talks with sensitivity, getting expert help, and building a supportive atmosphere are critical components of offering holistic support. As parents embark on this journey, it's vital to realise that resolving childhood depression is a collective effort involving both familial and professional assistance.

By combining knowledge, sensitivity, and a dedication to the child's well-being, parents can play a vital role in assisting their child's journey towards healing and resilience.

Chapter 8

<u>SUPPORTING YOUR OWN WELL-BEING</u>

When caring for a loved one suffering issues such as depression, it's tempting for caregivers to emphasise the well-being of their family member while neglecting their own. However, the caregiver's mental and emotional wellness is crucial to giving effective support.

This comprehensive resource addresses the necessity of self-care for the caregiver, strategies for recognizing and treating caregiver burnout, and the significance of seeking help and developing a strong network. By prioritising their own well-being, caregivers can preserve the stamina and resilience needed to handle the complexity of assisting a loved one during challenging times.

The Importance of Self-Care for the Caregiver

Self-care is not a luxury; it's a necessity, especially for those in caregiving duties. Caregivers often find themselves continually giving to others, and without purposeful attempts to recharge and care for their own well-being, they risk burnout and tiredness.

1. Prioritising Physical Health:

- Engage in regular physical activity that meets your tastes and ability. Whether it's a brisk walk, yoga, or a gym routine, physical exercise not only adds to physical health but also has significant impacts on mental well-being.

2. Nourishing Nutrition:

- Pay attention to your nutrition. Ensure that you are getting a balanced diet with a range of nutrients. Proper eating is vital for sustaining energy levels and general health.

3. Sufficient Rest:

- Prioritise sufficient and quality sleep. Lack of sleep can dramatically influence cognitive function, emotional well-being, and the ability to cope with stress.

4. Relaxation Techniques:

- Incorporate relaxation strategies into your routine, such as deep breathing exercises, meditation, or mindfulness. These routines can help decrease stress and generate a sense of serenity.

5. Establishing Boundaries:

- Set clear boundaries between your caregiving responsibilities and personal life. It's essential to carve out time for your own needs, hobbies, and activities that bring you joy.

6. Cultivating Hobbies:

- Engage in activities you love. Whether it's reading, gardening, or a creative pursuit, having hobbies outside of caregiving provides a valuable outlet for self-expression and enjoyment.

7. Regular Health Check-ups:
- Prioritise your own health by scheduling regular check-ups. As a caregiver, it's crucial to monitor and address any emerging health concerns promptly.

Recognizing and Managing Caregiver Burnout

Caregiver burnout is a state of physical, emotional, and mental exhaustion resulting from the prolonged and intense demands of caregiving. Recognizing the signs of burnout is crucial for taking proactive steps to manage and prevent its impact.

1. Signs of Caregiver Burnout:
- Physical Symptoms: Chronic fatigue, changes in sleep patterns, headaches, and increased susceptibility to illness.

- Emotional Exhaustion: Feelings of hopelessness, irritability, heightened anxiety, and a sense of being overwhelmed.
- Withdrawal from Activities: Loss of interest in activities that were once enjoyable, social withdrawal, and a diminished sense of accomplishment.
- Neglecting Personal Needs: Ignoring personal hygiene, inadequate self-care, and neglecting one's own well-being.

2. Strategies for Managing Caregiver Burnout:

- Acknowledge and Accept Your Feelings: It's okay to feel overwhelmed or stressed. Acknowledge your sentiments without judgement and acknowledge that it's a typical response to the challenges of caregiving.

- Seek Professional Guidance: Consider seeking the support of a mental health professional, such as a therapist or counsellor. Professional advice can provide coping methods and a secure space to explore and express your emotions.

- Delegate and Share Responsibilities: Don't hesitate to seek help and include others in caring responsibilities. Delegating responsibilities and sharing the caregiving role helps reduce some of the burdens and prevent burnout.

- Establish Realistic Expectations: Set realistic expectations for yourself. Understand that you cannot do everything, and it's alright to prioritise things and let go of perfectionism.

- Take Breaks and Respite: Schedule regular breaks and respite times. Whether it's a quick stroll, a coffee break, or a weekend away, spending time for oneself is vital for recharging.

- Join a Support Group: Connecting with other caregivers who understand your challenges can be incredibly validating and supportive. Joining a support group provides a space to share experiences, exchange advice, and receive emotional support.

- Utilise Respite Care Services: Explore respite care services that provide temporary relief for caregivers. This can involve professional caregivers coming in to assist or arranging for short-term stays in care facilities.

3. Preventing Caregiver Burnout:
- Prioritise Self-Care from the Beginning: Incorporate self-care practices into your routine from the outset of your caregiving journey. Prevention is key, and regular self-care can help build resilience against burnout.

- Communicate Openly with Your Loved One: Maintain open communication with the person you are caring for. Share your feelings, concerns, and the importance of maintaining a balance between caregiving and personal well-being.

- Stay Informed about Resources: Stay informed about available resources and support services in your community. Knowing where to turn for assistance can reduce stress and enhance your ability to provide effective care.

- Regularly Reevaluate Your Situation: Periodically reassess your caregiving situation. As the needs of the person you are caring for evolve, so should your approach to caregiving. Be open to adjusting your caregiving strategies as needed.

Seeking Support for Yourself and Fostering a Strong Support Network

Caregiving can be a challenging and isolating experience. Seeking support and fostering a strong network is essential for caregivers to navigate the emotional complexities of their role.

1. Identifying Sources of Support:
- Family and Friends: Reach out to family and friends for emotional support. Share your experiences, express your needs, and allow others to contribute to your well-being.

- Support Groups: Joining a support group for caregivers can provide a sense of community and understanding. It allows you to connect with others facing similar challenges and share insights and advice.

- Online Communities: Explore online communities and forums where caregivers share their experiences. Virtual platforms can be valuable for connecting with a diverse range of caregivers and accessing a wealth of shared knowledge.

- Mental Health Professionals: Consider seeking support from a mental health professional. Therapy or counselling provides a confidential space to explore your emotions, develop coping strategies, and receive personalised guidance.

- Community Resources: Explore local community resources and organisations that offer support for caregivers. These may include respite care services, educational programs, and assistance with navigating healthcare systems.

2. Fostering Effective Communication:

- Express Your Needs Clearly: Clearly explain your needs to people offering support. Whether it's identifying the type of service you require or conveying the emotional support you need, good communication is crucial.

- Educate Others about Caregiving complexities: Help individuals in your support network understand the complexities of caregiving. Educate them about the physical, emotional, and time needs required, building empathy and a better understanding.

- Regular Check-ins: Schedule regular check-ins with friends and family. These check-ins can give opportunity for open conversation, providing information, and addressing any evolving needs or issues.

3. The Role of Professional Support:
- Therapeutic Support: Engage in therapy or counselling to address the emotional toll of caregiving. A mental health expert can offer skills for coping, provide a non-judgmental space to express emotions, and support you in negotiating the intricacies of caregiving.

- Respite Care Services: Utilise respite care services to take breaks and refresh.

Professional caregivers can provide temporary relief, allowing you to attend to your personal needs without compromising the quality of care.

-        Consultation with Healthcare Professionals: Stay connected with the healthcare professionals involved in the care of your loved one. Regular consultations provide an opportunity to discuss any issues, gather information, and ensure that the care plan matches with the requirements of both the caregiver and the care recipient.

4. Building a Support Network:
- Diversify Your Network: Build a diversified support network that includes friends, family, professionals, and others who understand the particular challenges of caregiving. A diversified support system gives a diversity of perspectives and resources.

- Attend Workshops and Educational Programs: Attend workshops or educational programs about caregiving. These forums not only offer vital information but also provide opportunities to connect with other caregivers and establish a supportive community.

- Participate in Social Activities: Engage in social activities outside of the caregiving situation. Whether it's joining a club, attending community events, or participating in hobbies, social connections contribute to a well-rounded support network.

- Explore Online channels: Take use of online channels that link caregivers. Virtual communities give flexibility, allowing you to connect with others regardless of geographical boundaries.

5. Nurturing Reciprocal Relationships:

- Offer Reciprocal Support: Foster reciprocal ties within your support network. While it's necessary to receive help, delivering support to others fosters a sense of community and shared responsibility.

- Celebrate Achievements Together: Celebrate achievements, both great and small, with your support network. Acknowledging and sharing triumphs generates a good and inspiring environment.

6. The Impact of Support on Caregiver Well-being:

- Reducing Isolation: Support networks minimise the sensation of isolation typically experienced by caregivers. Knowing that people understand and empathise with your struggles increases emotional well-being.

- Giving Practical Assistance: Support networks can offer practical assistance, such as helping with errands, giving meals, or supplying respite care. These contributions alleviate the stress on the caregiver and promote a more sustainable caregiving dynamic.

- Enhancing Emotional Resilience: Emotional resilience is improved when caregivers feel supported and understood. Knowing that there is a network to turn to during hard times provides a significant buffer against stress.

- Encouraging Emotional Expression: A supportive network encourages caregivers to share their emotions openly. This emotional expression is crucial for mental health and prevents the accumulation of stress and dissatisfaction.

Supporting your own well-being as a caregiver is not a luxury—it's a crucial essential for giving effective and sustainable care. By prioritising their own well-being, caregivers can cultivate the strength and resilience needed to navigate the complexities of supporting a loved one through challenging times.

Remember, in the journey of caregiving, taking care of yourself is not selfish; it's an essential part of the caregiving process that ensures you can continue to provide the best possible care for your loved one while maintaining your own health and happiness.

Chapter 9

CELEBRATING PROGRESS AND RESILIENCE

In the challenging terrain of supporting a loved one through depression, acknowledging progress and cultivating resilience are vital components of the journey.

Acknowledging and Celebrating Small Victories

In the setting of depression, when the journey to recovery can be long, appreciating and celebrating minor achievements becomes a key element of the healing process. These modest wins may appear minor, but their impact on the individual's well-being and the overall trajectory of recovery is tremendous.

1. Defining Small Victories:
- Small wins comprise a range of achievements, from accomplishing a daily chore to conquering a specific problem connected with depression.
- Examples include getting out of bed in the morning, attending a social event, expressing feelings openly, or indulging in an enjoyable activity.

2. The Significance of Small Victories:
- Small successes contribute to a sense of accomplishment and growth, enhancing the individual's agency and resilience.
- They provide as physical evidence of the individual's capacity to handle problems and achieve significant strides, generating a positive feedback loop.

3. Celebrating Everyday Achievements:
- Encourage the celebration of everyday achievements. Recognize and applaud attempts to maintain habits, engage in

self-care, or take steps toward personal goals.

4. Shifting the Focus from Perfection to Progress:

- Emphasise progress over perfection. In the path from depression, the focus should be on the incremental strides ahead rather than an impossible quest of flawlessness.

5. The Cumulative Effect of Small Victories:

- Small triumphs, when compounded, lead to a sense of overall development and empowerment. The cumulative effect is transformative, altering the individual's sense of their ability to overcome obstacles.

6. The Role of Caregivers in Acknowledging Victories:

- Caregivers play a key role in identifying and applauding modest successes. Offer real appreciation, express pride in the individual's efforts, and actively participate in recognizing the significance of each achievement.

The Role of Resilience in the Journey Through Depression

Resilience is the capacity to bounce back from adversity, adapt to obstacles, and sustain well-being in the face of adversities. In the context of depression, resilience becomes a guiding force that encourages individuals to manage the ups and downs of their path with fortitude and tenacity.

1. Resilience as a Dynamic Process:

- Resilience is not a static trait but a dynamic process that evolves over time. It entails adapting to challenges, establishing coping mechanisms, and cultivating a happy mindset.

2. The Components of Resilience:

- Emotional Regulation: Resilience involves the ability to manage and regulate one's emotions in response to stressors. This includes recognizing and expressing emotions in a healthy manner.

- Adaptability: Resilience requires adaptability—the capacity to adjust and recalibrate in the face of changing circumstances and challenges.

- Positive Coping methods: Individuals with resilience adopt positive coping methods, such as seeking help, problem-solving, and maintaining a hopeful view.

- Self-Efficacy: Resilience is linked to self-efficacy, the belief in one's ability to effect positive change and overcome obstacles.

3. Nurturing Resilience in the Context of Depression:

- Encouraging Self-Reflection: Foster self-reflection to enhance self-awareness. Individuals can explore their strengths, values, and coping mechanisms, which form the foundation of resilience.

- Promoting Positive Thinking: Cultivate a positive mindset by concentrating on strengths, opportunities, and the potential for progress. Positive thinking adds to resilience in the face of hardship.

- Building a Supportive Network: Resilience is reinforced by a robust support network. Encourage the growth of meaningful ties with friends, family, and mental health experts.

- developing reasonable Goals: Assist folks in developing reasonable and achievable goals. Success in reaching these goals develops a sense of competence and resilience.

4. The Intersection of Resilience and Treatment:

- Resilience complements therapeutic interventions. It enhances the individual's ability to engage in treatment, implement coping strategies, and navigate the challenges inherent in the therapeutic process.

5. The Role of Caregivers in Fostering Resilience:

- Caregivers play a central role in fostering resilience. Offer unwavering support, actively engage in conversations about coping strategies, and reinforce the belief that recovery is an achievable and ongoing process.

<u>Looking Toward the Future with Hope and Optimism</u>

Hope is a powerful force that propels individuals forward, even in the darkest moments of depression. Cultivating hope involves envisioning a future that is not defined by the current struggles but is characterised by growth, recovery, and a renewed sense of purpose.

1. Shifting the Narrative from Despair to Possibility:

- Encourage a shift in the narrative from despair to possibility. Help individuals envision a future where their struggles are acknowledged but not defining, and where positive change is attainable.

2. The Impact of Hope on Mental Health:
- Hope contributes to mental well-being by providing a sense of purpose, motivation, and a belief in the potential for positive outcomes. It acts as a guiding light during challenging times.

3. Fostering a Sense of Agency:
- Cultivate a sense of agency by emphasising that individuals have the power to shape their own future. Empower them to make choices that align with their values and aspirations.

4. Setting Realistic Goals for the Future:
- Collaborate on setting realistic and achievable goals for the future. These goals can encompass various aspects of life, such

as relationships, career, personal growth, and overall well-being.

5. Navigating Uncertainty with Resilience:

- Acknowledge that the future is uncertain, and navigating this uncertainty requires resilience. Emphasise that setbacks are a natural part of the journey and can be overcome with time and perseverance.

6. The Role of Caregivers in Cultivating Hope:

- Caregivers play a crucial role in cultivating hope. Be a source of encouragement, reinforce positive changes, and communicate an unwavering belief in the individual's capacity for growth and recovery.

7. Professional Guidance in Shaping the Future:

- Collaborate with mental health professionals to shape a future-oriented treatment plan. Therapeutic interventions can focus on building skills, addressing underlying issues, and fostering a positive outlook.

8. The Connection Between Hope and Motivation:

- Hope is closely tied to motivation. Individuals with a sense of hope are more likely to engage in treatment, implement positive coping strategies, and actively participate in their journey toward recovery.

<u>Celebrating Progress and Resilience: A Holistic Approach</u>

Celebrating progress and fostering resilience are integral aspects of the holistic approach to navigating the journey through depression. This involves recognizing the interconnectedness of small victories, resilience, and hope in shaping a path toward well-being.

1. **The Interplay Between Small Victories and Resilience:**
- Small victories contribute to the development of resilience. Each accomplishment, no matter how modest, enhances the individual's belief in their ability to overcome challenges.

2. **Resilience as a Catalyst for Celebrating Progress:**
- Resilience functions as a catalyst for recognizing progress. It enables individuals to bounce back from failures, regard problems as chances for growth, and keep a forward-looking attitude.

3. **Hope as a Guiding Light in the Journey:**
- Hope serves as a guiding light that illuminates the journey through depression. It provides individuals with the motivation to persist, the belief in positive change, and the vision of a future imbued with possibilities.

4. The Role of Caregivers in the Holistic Approach:

- Caregivers play a vital role in developing a holistic strategy. By identifying and celebrating little triumphs, strengthening resilience, and fostering hope, caregivers contribute considerably to the overall well-being of their loved ones.

Celebrating progress and resilience in the road through depression is a dynamic and continuing process that takes intention, compassion, and a conviction in the potential for good change.

By embracing these characteristics, individuals and their support networks may traverse the complexity of depression with a feeling of purpose and resilience.

The road is unique for each person, but with the correct support, an unflinching belief in one's capacity for progress, and a willingness to celebrate even the tiniest steps forward, the path toward recovery becomes more navigable and transformative.

CONCLUSION

The process of loving someone with depression is hard, demanding, and frequently transformational. As we reflect on the struggles and accomplishments, the highs and lows, it becomes obvious that this road is not linear, but rather a dynamic exploration of emotions, resilience, and compassion.

1. **Embracing the Complexity of the Journey:**

- The journey is marked by its complexity, encompassing moments of deep connection, understanding, and love, alongside the challenges of navigating the impact of depression on both individuals in the relationship.

2. The Significance of Connection and Understanding:

- Connection and understanding form the bedrock of this journey. Through open communication, empathy, and a commitment to mutual support, partners can develop a durable bond that weathers the storms of depression.

3. The Unpredictability of Depression:

- Depression is inherently unpredictable. Its ebbs and flows can defy expectations, and the journey may involve periods of progress followed by setbacks. Understanding this unpredictability is essential for maintaining a sense of perspective.

4. The Role of Patience and Perseverance:

- Patience and perseverance emerge as guiding virtues. Loving someone with depression requires a steadfast commitment to weathering the challenges together, recognizing that healing is a gradual and ongoing process.

5. The Impact on Both Partners:
- Acknowledging the impact of depression on both partners is crucial. While one may be directly navigating the symptoms, the other grapples with the emotional weight of supporting their loved one. Both experiences are valid, and both partners need support.

6. Moments of Connection and Resilience:
- Amidst the hardships, there are moments of connection and perseverance that underline the power of the partnership. Celebrating these moments, no matter how tiny, becomes a source of inspiration and motivation.

7. The Dual Role of Caregiver and Partner:

- Partners often find themselves managing the dual position of caregiver and life partner. Striking a balance between offering support and maintaining a romantic connection involves open communication and mutual understanding.

8. The Transformative Power of Love:

- Love, in its truest form, is a transformational power. It becomes the guiding light that inspires both partners to learn, grow, and navigate the complexities of depression with grace, compassion, and unwavering support.

<u>Encouraging Ongoing Learning and Growth</u>

The road of loving someone with depression is not stagnant but a constant evolution that enables both partners to engage in continuing learning and improvement. This process is defined by self-discovery, increased communication skills, and a greater awareness of mental health.

1. The Value of Self-Reflection:
- Ongoing learning begins with self-reflection. Partners are encouraged to explore their own beliefs, assumptions, and coping processes. This self-awareness forms the foundation for effective communication and support.

2. Enhancing Communication Skills:
- Communication is the lifeblood of any relationship, especially when facing the hardships of depression. Ongoing learning involves sharpening communication skills, creating empathy, and responding to the growing requirements of each partner.

3. Educating Yourself on Depression:
- Knowledge is a strong instrument. Partners are advised to educate themselves about depression, its many forms, and the available treatment choices. This

information helps them to navigate the trip with educated compassion.

4. Navigating the Nuances of Treatment:

- The landscape of mental health care is always shifting. Partners are asked to be updated about new advancements, treatment techniques, and therapeutic approaches. This awareness permits them to actively participate in the therapy experience.

5. Cultivating Emotional Intelligence:

- Emotional intelligence is a cornerstone of effective support. Partners can boost their emotional intelligence by having a knowledge of their own emotions and those of their loved one. This cultivates a sympathetic and empathetic connection.

6. Seeking Support for Both Partners:

- The path is not designed to be navigated alone. Both spouses gain from obtaining support—individually and as a couple. This may involve treatment, support groups, or connecting with mental health resources customised to their individual needs.

7. Embracing Flexibility and Adaptability:

- Growth typically needs flexibility and adaptability. Partners are encouraged to embrace change, adapt to new situations, and face issues with a collaborative perspective. This adaptability enhances the resilience of the partnership.

8. Nurturing Personal Passions and Interests:

- Ongoing learning extends beyond the field of mental health. Partners are encouraged to follow their passions and interests. Cultivating individual growth helps to a better and more rewarding partnership.

A Message of Hope for Both Partners in the Relationship

In the middle of the challenges inherent in loving someone with depression, a message of hope becomes a beacon pointing both partners toward the prospect of recovery, growth, and a future filled with shared joy.

1. A Testament to Resilience:

- The very path of loving someone with depression is a testimonial to the strength of both parties. It is an appreciation of the strength to face misfortune together and emerge stronger on the other side.

2. The Power of Connection:

- The power of connection cannot be underestimated. Despite the darkness of sadness, the bond between couples remains a source of light, love, and unshakable support. This relationship is a lifeline that transcends the hardships.

3. The Transformative Nature of Love:
- Love, when fostered and sustained, has the potential to transform. It converts problems into chances for growth, despair into hope, and the journey into a shared narrative of strength, perseverance, and success.

4. Embracing the Imperfect Perfection:
- Imperfection is an integral component of the human experience. Partners are urged to appreciate the flawed perfection of their connection. The path is not about obtaining an ideal state but about managing hurdles with sincerity and love.

5. The Beauty of Shared Growth:
- Growth is a joint endeavour. As both partners commit to continuing learning, personal development, and supporting one other's individual journeys, they contribute to the beauty of shared growth within the relationship.

6. Celebrating the Uniqueness of Each Journey:

- Every journey through depression is unique. Partners are reminded to celebrate the uniqueness of their path. It is a tapestry weaved with both struggles and achievements, creating a narrative that is completely theirs.

7. The Endurance of Hope:

- Hope endures even in the darkest moments. It is a flame that flickers but never extinguishes. Partners are taught to hold onto hope, recognizing it as a driving force that pulls them ahead, even when the route looks uncertain.

8. The Promise of Tomorrow:

- Tomorrow provides the promise of new beginnings. Partners are encouraged to look toward the future with optimism, picturing a tomorrow that is moulded by shared dreams, perseverance, and the unshakeable sense that, together, they can conquer any difficulty.

In ending the investigation of the road of loving someone with depression, it is evident that this path is a powerful and transformational experience. It demands for resilience, compassion, and an everlasting commitment to growth.

As partners reflect on the obstacles they've experienced, engage in continual learning, and embrace a message of optimism, they are not only navigating a journey—they are actively constructing a shared story of love, understanding, and triumph over adversity. In the fabric of relationships, the threads of compassion, connection, and hope build a mosaic that portrays the enduring beauty of love in its most real form.